Spandex-Optional Bicycle Touring

How to ride long distance, the cheap and easy way

PETER RICE

A Dog Tooth Paperback
Albuquerque, New Mexico

Cover design by Anne Bean. Illustrations by Lindsay Wood.

ISBN–13: 978-1500959333
ISBN–10: 1500959332
Library of Congress Control Number: 2014911720

Printed in the United States of America

For Tajique, New Mexico

CONTENTS

"Make voyages! Attempt them. There's nothing else."
—Tennessee Williams

MANIFESTO

THE IMPORTANT THING is to ride. Remember that. And don't let anyone tell you otherwise.

To look at the bicycle touring world from the outside is to take a confusing and overwhelming punch to the gut. It's full of ludicrously expensive bikes, equally expensive flashy gear of dubious necessity, and a lifestyle that involves some really bizarre twists on conventional reality. In this world, "food" comes in small foil packets. Tires are so strong that they can double as armor for tanks. And really, what's up with all the Spandex?

Is this intimidating tableau truly necessary? No. The subculture surrounding tricked out gear and accessories is great as far as it goes, but the important thing is to ride, and to enjoy yourself in the meantime.

This book is for the rest of us: People who like to ride bikes around town, but who might also want to ride them over to the next county, the next state, or across the country — without mortgaging the house or becoming a mechanical engineer in the process.

Bicycle touring is a truly great way to spend a few days, a few weeks, or a few months. You get to see beautiful scenery, meet interesting people, and experience America in a unique way: Slowly, while nursing the mother of all endorphin rushes. On a deeper level, you get to know yourself. Bicycle touring is the perfect marriage of straight up fun and deeply spiritual introspection.

I've been doing occasional tours for several years now — pretty much whenever I can get some time off work. I've logged about 4,000 miles worth of tour, so far covering every Western state except Nevada and Wyoming. But let me be clear: I am no Superman, no candidate for an Under Armour commercial. I could stand to lose about 20 pounds. I hate running. Hiking bores me to death. I know I should do yoga but I don't. I am not a member of a gym. I generally don't buy organic food. I do not recall ever drinking a protein shake, though Tang really does hit the spot sometimes.

For the most part, I ride bikes that mechanics would turn their noses up at. The bike I rode down the Oregon Coast was such a piece of junk that I seriously considered leaving it out to be stolen at my destination, rather than paying more than it was worth to ship it home. I have never toured with a bike whose age could not be measured in decades.

Why? Because the important thing is to ride. The important thing is to be in halfway decent shape and motivated to keep going.

I say all this because bicycle tourists are often looked on by others as minor gods. The sheer distances involved, the outrageous costumes, the unexplored questions about where exactly one sleeps — people look at this and somehow think they are not worthy. I like to be the recipient of awestruck praise as much as the next guy, but in the interest of full disclosure, I don't deserve it. You really are worthy. The only difference between those who tour by bicycle and those who don't is a plan, and a bit of training. This book will help you come up with that plan.

Mind you, this book is not a comprehensive guide to get you prepared for everything. If that were even possible to write, it would be a terrible read. The goal here is to get you prepared enough, and where words on a page fail, you will be directed to a YouTube video, an expert salesman, or a friend. This book is a briefing, not a hand-holding exercise. It assumes that you can ride a bike, know what to do around cars, can handle a few logistical challenges, and can enlist your friends or the web in a few basic research projects.

Tours come in all shapes and sizes. Some are supported and catered by companies or non-profits, and you'll never be far from a van that can bail you out. Some are supported and catered by loving and understanding spouses, and you must make a special effort to impress them next Valentine's Day. Other tours are completely self-supported, with all gear packed onto the bike. That's my favorite style of bike travel, but it's also the most complicated and therefore best spelled out in a book.

Whichever option you go with, it will prove to be an exercise in improvisation. No matter how much you prepare, there will always be new challenges to ponder and new problems to troubleshoot. That's part of the appeal: No journey will be exactly like the last.

THERE'S QUITE A LOT OF STERN TALK in this book, and with good reason: Like driving, hockey, basketball, or even sitting on the couch all day eating potato chips, bicycle touring is not without risks, and you deserve a direct, plain-spoken assessment of what they are and how to minimize them.

Still, you also deserve to know that bicycle touring is bigger than life, when done right. Ride around town and you'll enjoy a perfectly pleasant method of commuting, visiting friends, running errands, or generally killing time. Ride around a country road for an afternoon, and you'll get some quality exercise and clear your mind for a few hours. But go on a tour, and you'll change your life.

Every day, you probably practice a well-established routine. You go to work at the same job, spend time with the same people, sleep in the same bed and eat the same food. And there's nothing wrong with this. It's how we built our great civilization, after all.

But there comes a time when these routines must be broken: A time to tap into a more primal side. A time to seek adventure and freedom. A time to mimic, as practically as we possibly can in a modern era, what it must have been like for our ancestors to set off into the wilderness, away from everything familiar, alone. A time to live by our wits, and to trust our gut. And a time to connect with ourselves, even as we disconnect from others.

That's bicycle touring. To say that it is merely fun diminishes its true power — like saying the sun is just a source of light. Touring is transcendent, spiritual, epic. It's like falling in love, or the first time you saw a big city at night out the window of a plane, or a sunset over the ocean. It is whatever grandiose words you use in a failed attempt to describe something that should probably just be experienced. It is everything a vacation should be.

You may go on a tour, and finish it in a flash of glory, but you can't truly go home again, because the world will look just a bit different. And perhaps the next time you find yourself mired in a bothersome routine, you will remember the feats of greatness you experienced on tour, and you will smile a little knowing smile to yourself. Touring is hard, but it's a beautiful hard.

And if that doesn't appeal to you, check this out: On tour, you can eat whatever you want and you'll probably still lose weight.

Anyway, see you out there.

Peter Rice
Albuquerque, New Mexico
July, 2014

JERRY THE BIKE MECHANIC

 Jerry Beaupré is the proprietor of Beaupré Bodacious Bicycles in Albuquerque. He is a one-man cheerleading squad for bicycle riding, and he could care less how much you paid for your wheels, so long as you are putting miles on them. He is also the bicycling world's answer to a Havana car mechanic: A frugal champion of old gear, a man who would take function over form any day of the week, and a man dedicated to squeezing every last ounce of life out of every single part. Beaupré acted as a consultant for this book, and his input can be found all over these pages, whether quoted directly or not.

THE TOKEN GEAR CHAPTER

YOU MAY HAVE heard about bikes that are specifically designed for touring. Take this with a grain of salt. There is no objectively perfect touring bike out there, because bicycling is much more like a relationship or religion than an engineering problem. You just need to find a bike that you can get along with. And if it leaves you in a state of transcendent awe, so much the better. The only perfect bike is a bike you like to ride. If you get your bike straight from the Trek factory and pay for it with $5,000 worth of gold bullion, great. If you get it for $20 at a garage sale, also great. So long as you like to ride it, it's perfect.

This bike you like to ride needs two more things: Water bottle holders (get those at a bike shop or big box store) and some capacity to haul stuff. For that you have three options:

Cargo Option One: Saddle Bags (Panniers)

This is the most popular choice with road riders, since it's cheaper and almost always lighter than Option Two. Saddle bags attach to either side of your back rack, leaving convenient room on top to strap down additional stuff. (I put my deflated air mattress and sleeping bag into the sort of dry bag used by river rafters and then lash it to the rack.)

Racks often come standard on the backs of bicycles, but the version for the front, along with the special front-mounted bags, is usually another purchase. Expect to pay between $35 and $50 for racks. Not all bikes can accommodate racks, so have a mechanic evaluate your bike if you are not already set up.

Top-of-the-line front saddle bags can be bought new for something in the $150 neighborhood, while back bags sell for about $250. Bags in this price range are truly awesome. They will lock themselves to your rack and never let go even if the bike is turned upside down. They are also waterproof (usually) and built like tanks. If, however, you can live without these features, you will be able to find saddle bags for under $100, if not under $50. Check bike shops or online venues like eBay. Some riders also use a bag that is attached to the handle bars, for those who must maximize carrying capacity. Those bags often feature clear plastic pockets through which you can read a map.

While I admit to drooling at the sight of a sick saddle bag, mine are, in fact, not waterproof, not built like tanks, and will come unhooked if I hit a particularly nasty bump. And they were especially cheap, since I more-or-less stole them from my parents. I cannot recommend this method of gear acquisition highly enough.

Cargo Option Two: Trailers

These are popular with off-road riders because adding a lot of weight directly to your bike in the form of saddle bags is bound to be awkward when jostling around a hillside. Trailers come in all shapes and sizes and cost hundreds of dollars for the new top-of-the-line varieties. (Some even have shock absorbers, which you may want to consider if you're traveling on particularly shocking terrain.) Of course, you can get them cheap online or even make one yourself. Check the Internet or local bike shop to learn more.

I once ran into a bike tourist in northern New Mexico who towed a simple platform trailer to which he had attached one of those big plastic tubs that people buy in the midst of a garage organization frenzy. He fit all of his stuff in that tub, including a golf cart battery that powered a portable DVD player. He charged the battery with a 70s-era solar panel roped (roped!) to the top of the tub. Let this anonymous bike tourist, probably watching DVDs at a poached campsite somewhere right now, serve as inspiration for us all.

They add weight, but trailers have the practical advantage of being easy to get rid of. If you arrive at your campsite and then want to go somewhere else without all your stuff, trailers will make that happen easily.

Cargo Option Three: Backpacks

I've heard of people doing this, but it can't be very common. It will make for a very sweaty back, but if you can fit everything you need in a pack, more power to you. Especially if it's a short trip or you are staying in motels the whole time and don't need to bring bedding, this could be very feasible.

BIKES

Three main bicycle types dominate the universe: Mountain, road, and hybrid. All three can be used for touring, but there are advantages and disadvantages to consider. Let's review them.

Mountain Bikes

These are easy to distinguish because they have handle bars shaped like a "T." They are designed for unpaved roads and trails.

Advantages: Upright position is comfortable. Thick and often knobby tires make navigating bumps, potholes, and unpaved roads a snap. Gears are biased toward the easy side of the spectrum, which is great if you are riding up a steep trail.

Disadvantages: Upright position increases wind resistance against your body. Thick tires increase friction, translating into fewer miles ridden at the end of the day. Easy gears mean riding on paved roads will take more effort than with other bikes.

Road Bikes

These feature handle bars that look like the horns of a ram. They are designed for going fast on paved roads, and are the most popular choice with bicycle tourists. Touring bikes are a subset of this category. The primary difference with those is a larger wheel base (the distance between the points where the two tires touch the ground) that stabilizes the bike, even if it is carrying a lot of extra weight.

Advantages: The design forces you to lean over, minimizing wind resistance. Road bikes are generally the lightest of the three classes. Gear design is biased toward speed, so even when going downhill you can keep up and usually go even faster. With thin slick tires pumped up to a high pressure, you will minimize friction with the road.

Disadvantages: The rider must lean very far forward — hunched over, really — and that takes some getting used to. It's a bit harder to steer. Lightness is great but if you are hauling a lot of heavy stuff you may want something more solid. Gear design means hills will be a little more challenging. With thin, high pressure tires you will feel every bump in the road. If you ever need to go on an unpaved road, you may have to walk or go very slowly.

Hybrids

These bikes split the difference between road and mountain designs in a bunch of different ways. You might have a hybrid with road bike gears and mountain bike handle bars, for instance. Different bikes may emphasize different factors that you may or may not care about.

Advantages: Better chance of splitting the difference in a way you like.

Disadvantages: Constantly having to explain what a hybrid is. Also, finding exactly what you like.

Whatever bike you choose — even if it's something completely off the wall like a single-gear or a unicycle — make sure it conforms to your standards of reliability. If you expect your bike to be built like a tank and to run like a Swiss watch, make sure it is/does. If you think that breaking down is just part of the adventure, then you can adjust accordingly (And we'll see you at the garage sales this weekend!). More on this in the troubleshooting chapter on page 70.

While these three categories encompass the vast majority of bikes on the market, segmentation within the categories is happening even as we speak. Thirty years ago, bikes were like TV channels: Few choices, but appealing to a large audience. These days, they are still like TV channels: there are many, and they appeal to niche audiences. There may be one type of bike that is specifically designed for a particular terrain, a particular body type, or people born under Sagittarius when Neptune was waxing. If you enjoy this sort of detail, welcome to the modern world. But frankly, it makes me go cross eyed, so I'll be sticking to the "ride it if you like it" philosophy.

One more word about bikes: If you have a tricked-out custom bike, congratulations. You may have problems, however, if you break down in the middle of nowhere. Some types of spare bike parts are stocked at nearly every shop in this great land. Others, not so much. Ask your mechanic.

(Finding a bike mechanic, by the way, is just like finding a car mechanic. Try a few out, get recommendations from friends, go with what makes you comfortable.)

TIRES

Now that you have your bike type chosen, your rack situation squared away, and the great saddle-bag-versus-trailer debate settled, it's time to focus on your tires. Getting a flat tire is about the most common bike problem you're going to encounter, and you should know what to do when you get one. The second best way to learn how to change or patch them is to ask a friend to show you or get the directions from a YouTube video. But the best way to learn is to break down on the side of the road without a cell phone, 20 miles from the nearest bike shop yet with all the parts you need for the job. I find circumstances like this efficiently focus the mind to the task at hand, but that could just be me. Either way, learn it.

If you want to avoid repairs as much as possible you need to re-enforce your tires somehow. And here you have many options:

1. **Tires** are not created equal. Some are old, thin, or mangy. Others are solid as rocks yet still flexible. Basic tires can usually be had for about $20, but spending a lot of money ($60-$80 per tire) on a strong set will avoid most flats. The disadvantage is that if you run over a razor blade — let's just say that in that department, all tires are created equal. Some tires are made specifically for touring. They are harder and last longer, but sacrifice performance. But trust me on this: You can get pretty far with 20-year-old junk rejected by Jerry the Bike Mechanic's more discerning clients.

2. **Inner-tubes** come in a thin conventional variety, but also a much thicker "thorn-resistant" class that can stop most punctures before they start. If you live in a part of the country cursed by thorned goatheads or blackberry bushes, these thicker tires should be easy to find. If not, you may have to look a little harder or go online. They work well and hold air much longer than their conventional cousins, but they do add weight and are harder to install.

3. **Tire sealant** is a thick liquidish goo that you can shoot into your inner-tubes to prevent flats. (The most common brand is Slime, which is easy to spot thanks to its neon green color.) If

you get a puncture the goo usually fills up the hole and stops the leak. Sometimes you can even hear this process happening, which is way beyond cool. But in much the same way that a hardboiled egg spins more easily than the raw variety, the sealant inhibits the rolling motion of the wheel, which is not even approaching cool. Still, not bad if you may, at some point, ride through a field of cactus.

4. **Tire liners** act as an effective buffer between the tube and the tire. Sometimes they are made of Kevlar or other impressive-sounding substances. Expect to pay dearly for these, especially if the name evokes something that would impress a United States Marine. But beware: A $40 tire is better than a $20 tire combined with a $20 liner. There is something to be said for simplicity and elegance.

You'll want to choose some combination of the preceding based on how you personally balance the value of going fast with the value of saving money and the value of not having to fix flats or change tires very often. On one end of the spectrum are people who live on the edge, going with the cheap tires and thin tubes. In fact, you may be able to ride for many hundreds of miles without incident in some parts of the country doing this. On the other end of the spectrum, you could get nice tires, a liner, and thorn resistant tubes with sealant. You could run over an improvised explosive device with that and be fine. If that sort of overkill helps you sleep at night, we're with you.

No matter what bike or tire or cargo arrangement you choose, however, keep in mind that the most important part of a bike is the engine, also known as you. That crack about touring on a unicycle or a single gear was only half joking. You could do it. It's possible. So long as the wheels are more-or-less intact, the only thing you have to worry about is putting one foot in front of the other.

The Great Schrader v. Presta Debate

The valves on tubes come in a thick, short variety called Schrader (also found on most car tires) and a thin long variety called Presta. Both hold air just fine and are reasonably easy to pump up (though make sure your pump is compatible with what you have). Schrader has market penetration going for it. If a department store in Anytown, USA stocks only one tire, it'll probably be Schrader. But the best wheels are made for Presta. Pay your money and take your choice.

 TIP FROM JERRY: Tire liners, thorn resistant tubes, sealants — these are nothing but scandalous wastes of money! All you need is "The System," a low-tech but very effective method of flat prevention. Take an old tire that is slightly smaller than your current one, and cut the edges off. (By edges we mean the first 1/8 inch or so of edge if you were able to lay the tire flat. This is the part that contains a tense metal wire, known as the "bead," that gives the tire strength and shape.) Then stuff that beadless old tire it in your new tire. Use baby powder to grease the skids if that's proving difficult. It's the perfect liner: Free, recycled, and just as effective as those $80 tires. The only puny drawback is that it adds the weight of the old tire. Best of all, since you effectively have two tires, your outer tire can be a complete piece of crap! Ride it into the ground and laugh all the way to the bank!

PEDALS

Normal pedals will work just fine for long rides, but many cyclists choose to essentially lock their feet to the pedals, allowing them to move the bike along the entire circular motion — not just the downward part. You have two options for this locking mechanism.

Clips

These look like open-ended cages for your toes. Stick your street shoes in there and pedal away! Available at bike shops and online.

Advantages: You can use normal shoes (except perhaps large boots). They are also cheap and can often be attached to existing pedals. You don't have to know much about bikes or be very handy to install them yourself.

Disadvantages: They are not as slick or efficient as the following option.

Clipless pedals

Special shoes attach to special pedals by way of a special "cleat."

Advantages: There is no more efficient way to convert your energy into forward motion. You will probably notice a double digit percentage improvement over option one.

Disadvantages: Getting set up could easily cost you $250. Part of the process will involve precision adjustments to the components, taking into account how you normally point your feet, which type of shoe is best for you, and how to fit it just right. Count on a long conversation with your mechanic about all this. Also, it's worth mentioning that you will probably be ruined for life. Option one or, God forbid, regular pedals, will forever be inferior.

WHY TRAINING SUCKS

TRAINING — the process of getting ready for whatever trip you've got cooked up — is a tough pill to swallow. Keeping to a rigorous schedule that involves a lot of sweating is a huge pain. It makes bike riding feel like work, which is a drag and flirts with being counterproductive. Training, in short, sucks, and I don't generally recommend it.

In fact, I myself do not really train, per se. The only time I can get myself to ride a bike is when I (1.) need to get somewhere, (2.) want to hang out with a friend and propose a bike ride as a good way to do it, or (3.) when an element of adventure and discovery is hanging over my head.

The prospect of going out for a ride and returning to the same place a couple of hours later is rarely enough to get me out of the house. (There was this one time when, living in Mexico without a bike, I took a spinning class to stay in shape for a planned 1,000-mile ride. But in my defense, the class was full of attractive women.)

If by some miracle of genetics or circumstance you have the sort of personality it takes to train, I recommend setting escalating goals for yourself. Start by doing whatever you can, be it 500 feet or fifty miles. Keep doing it and keep challenging yourself to do more until you can go a distance that is, say, 30 percent longer than the distance between supply stops and/or campsites on your proposed trip route.

For the other 95 percent of humanity, I recommend an alternative strategy: Work bicycle riding into your daily routine, then plan a realistic trip that doubles as a ramped up training schedule.

Every Day Biking: The Odysseus Model

Motivation is a rather fleeting thing, and crumples when faced with an easy out. If you don't believe me just visit a gym during the first week of January and then the first week of July. You'll see which New Year's resolutions stuck, and the many more that ended up collecting dust in the back cupboards of our minds.

The trick to motivation is to follow the example of Odysseus, the hero of Homer's epic *The Odyssey*. He was motivated to get home to the lovely Penelope but knew his self-discipline would crumple when faced with the sirens, who in this parable represent sitting at home on your couch, driving, Twinkies, or whatever else is standing between you and your bike. He knew that given the option of an easy out, he would take it.

So he removed the easy out in advance. He ordered his men to tie him to the mast, still able to hear the siren call but unable to do anything about it. Odysseus was a smart dude.

This is the best way to get yourself to ride a bike on a regular basis: Remove all other options. Give the car keys to your teenager. Park your car at a friend's house across town, or better yet, sell it. Forbid family members from giving you rides except in cases of emergency or illness. Start riding to work and then devote the savings to paying for something you would rather have than a comfortable, exertion-free commute. Give some money to a friend of an offensive political persuasion, then tell him or her to donate $10 to some ridiculous cause every time you chicken out and drive. In short, do whatever you have to do to structurally readjust your life to make room for regular bike time.

Not only will this be good for your health, it will be good for getting you in shape for some serious touring. Every Saturday here in Albuquerque you'll see an army of Spandex-clad cyclists hitting the trails. It's a good thing, to be sure. But if you ride 10 miles per day just getting to work and back, you're probably ahead of those weekend warriors in terms of mileage.

Besides, riding a bike to work or for errands saves time. You have to get to work one way or another, and you have to ride a bike one way or another. If you combine the two you'll save as much time as you would have spent driving.

This is not to say that going for long rides on the weekend is a bad idea. Ideally, you would do it all the time in preparation for your trip. At a minimum, though, do it a few times. Get up in the morning and ride until you can't ride anymore. The self-knowledge gained will be useful in making the many judgment calls demanded by the open road.

Realistic Planning: What Floats Your Boat

Whatever regular bike riding regimen you come up with, you'll soon start to get a feel for what you're capable of. Plan your trip while taking into account that, plus where exactly you will be touring and what exactly you want to get out of this experience.

If you can handle 30 miles per week of commuting but not much more, you may want to tour in a densely populated part of the country, with towns and places to stay every 15 miles or so. Think Iowa farm country, or along the coasts. That's not a hardcore tour, and you may have the time of your life anyway.

But if you clear 100 miles per week with no problem, you may be able to handle biking through rural Utah, where the next water source — to say nothing of a town — might be 50 miles away. That's hardcore, and you may be capable of it, but there's no guarantee you'll enjoy it. Do what you enjoy, even if you use a unicycle and go five miles per day.

Either way, you should consider the first few days of the trip to be part of your training — all the training you swore you would do but never got around to. This is the time to ramp up and get in your zone, whatever that may be. Plan some easy days, then mid-range, then reach for the high mileage days.

Reasonably healthy people with decent motivation will get in really good shape really fast during the first few days because the mindset of a ride is totally different than the mindset of normal day-to-day life. On the road, it's real, and you have nothing else to think about. Push through those aches and pains, and on the other side you'll be able to dramatically increase your daily mileage.

My informal survey of fellow tourists reveals that 40-60 miles per day is about average if you're going on paved roads. But you really shouldn't pay any attention to that. This is your tour, and only you can make the call as to why you're doing it in the first place. I like to clear 500 miles per week and will save time by eating cold food from convenience stores to pull it off. But in his ideal world, Jerry the Bike Mechanic would go 20-30 miles per day, arrive at a town, make two or three friends, then invite them all over to his campsite for a gourmet dinner. If there happened to be a music festival passing through that town a few days hence, he would stick around for it.

Some people tour to see what they are capable of. Some people tour because it's a good way to meet interesting people. Some people tour because food tastes better after a long bike ride. There is no one way to do this. There is only your way. All you have to do is figure out what that is and plan (or in Jerry's case, don't plan) accordingly.

Stuff You Should Know How to Do

Training for a tour is about much more than learning to ride a bike for an unusually long distance. You'll want to learn a few critical outdoor survival skills as well.

1. **Be comfortable camping**. Figure out what kind of weather you'll be biking through, and then get used to the idea of sleeping outside in it, all while defending your food supply from the local wildlife. Most bike tourists camp along the way, if only because it's about the cheapest option out there. (Skip this step if you plan to stay in motels the whole time — "credit card" touring. And while you skip this step, know that I am jealous.) If you are biking in desolate rural areas where campgrounds are few and far between, you should be comfortable camping without the benefit of the services found at campgrounds, such as water. Which leads us to...

2. **Be comfortable going to the bathroom** without the benefit of an outhouse or flush toilet. Depending on where you are biking, you may never need to employ these skills, but they are good to know anyway.

3. **Learn how much water you need** at different temperatures. When on tour, especially in arid climates, you will always be making judgement calls about when to fill up on water. You need to get to a point where you can look at your water supply and accurately translate it into miles ridden. Nothing will screw up your trip more than a case of dehydration. At best, you'll have to drink some rather foul tasting concentrated electrolyte. (Available at drug stores and the bigger grocery stores.) At worst, you die. Know what you're capable of and don't push it.

4. **Ride in every condition imaginable** and get used to it. On tour you will be at the mercy of the elements. Some of these elements, such as ice storms, may be your cue to find the nearest motel and lay low for a while. For others, like rain, stopping the tour may not be a good option. Learn what you can handle in terms of rain and wind and sun. Put yourself in a few imperfect biking situations and then get through them. Do the same while

carrying some extra weight on your bike. This is true training. It's also a commercial for the benefits of commuting to work by bike. Ride to work every day for a year and you'll probably end up well conditioned to a wide temperature range and every conceivable type of weather. Unless of course you live in Florida, in which case you will at least have experience touring in hurricane-force winds.

5. **Have a plan for dogs**. Riding through new areas always carries the danger of an unfortunate encounter with a dog. Usually they just want to raise a ruckus and look menacing, rather than maim you, but you don't want to take any chances. Every situation is different, but generally you have the following options: (1.) Outrun them. This is the best option if available. (2.) Get off your bike as fast as possible, put your bike between yourself and the dog, then inch away from the scene, all the while looking and feeling as menacing as you can. Reach down to the ground and pretend to pick up a rock that you then pretend to throw. Or, if a real rock is available, use that. Hopefully the ruckus will attract the dog's owner and the situation will resolve itself. (3.) Carry dog spray, a Louisville Slugger, taser gun, real gun, or other weapon and know how to use it. (I just use the first two options and have never been bitten.) Spraying water at dogs also works sometimes.

6. **Get over your fear of hills**. Most people have an irrational fear of hills, as though they are some great physical difficulty. In my experience, though, they are 80 percent psychological. Any bike with a decent gear assembly will take most or all of the physical hardship out of a hill. (But you may want to reconsider that single-gear model if you're crossing the Rockies.) Still, you're exerting yourself more and not getting much distance to show for it, which is hard. Often in life we're faced with hard tasks that we just need to buckle down and accomplish. Whatever strategy you use for those, try it out on hills. (Mine is distraction and looking at the bright side: I crank up some tunes and take in the scenery while trying to enjoy the adrenaline, the generally

negligible wind, and the height-enhanced FM radio reception.) However you do it, learn to go along and get along with hills.

Training, as mentioned above, sucks. There's no way around it. To make sure your tour doesn't end before it begins, be realistic when it comes to training expectations. Don't set yourself up for failure. And if you look to be headed for failure anyway, just redefine what success is. (This applies to much of life, by the way.) Lower your daily mileage quota if you have to. The last thing you want is to develop a deep-seated loathing for riding, so make it as much fun as you can. Riding is more important than how much you ride.

Long-haul bicyclists will never be mistaken for NBA stars. They're just people who keep going. The sooner you recognize that, the sooner you will feel comfortable joining our imperfect ranks.

PLANNING YOUR ROUTE

IN THE UNITED STATES, bicycles are allowed to use the same roads as cars with a few limited exceptions. For example, cities may have dismount zones in pedestrian-heavy downtown areas. Many interstate highways are also off limits. Each state has different rules, and it never hurts to check in with your local law enforcement authorities, but generally, if you can go there in a Honda Civic, you can go there on a bike.

That said, the type of road makes a big difference. Depending on your personal style, you may prefer one over another, and knowing the details will help you plan.

Unpaved county, Forest Service, BLM, or generally very rural roads

You're worried about traffic on these roads? Stop. Worry instead about whether it is impolite not to wave to your fellow auto-encapsulated travelers. Worry also about having a good map. Gas station maps are great, but they don't help you much in the hinterlands.

Paved county, Forest Service, BLM, or otherwise rural roads

You probably have little to fear except cattle guards on these roads. The lack of shoulder is usually made up for by the lack of traffic. Some of these roads won't see a car for hours on end. Drivers in big cities must take care to avoid pedestrians, other cars, billboards, medians, etc. Drivers on these roads, however, don't have much to distract them. So even without all the normal road fixins, I feel pretty safe.

Municipal Bike Paths

These can be awesome and infuriating all in the same day. Generally, bike paths (as opposed to *lanes* on city streets) take you through all sorts of fun and scenic terrain. They can be a God-send when navigating through a dense urban area. Finding them, however, can be a serious pain, even with the advent of bicycling directions on Google Maps.

Like most bicycling infrastructure across this great land, paths are often poorly labeled. It's hard to know where you are and where you are going, whether the path will be closed for repairs around the next bend, or whether a paved trail will stay that way. I've found the best way to pick up intelligence on this is to find a local bike person who knows what they're doing. Some cities and private groups also publish maps, and it couldn't hurt to do some research ahead of time. Bike shops will be a good resource for this.

City Streets

A real crap shoot. Some are quiet and calm with bike lanes. Others you wouldn't want to be caught dead on. Even small towns out in the middle of nowhere can have gnarly main drags. Often you can just take side streets to avoid this. In big cities, where there are many main drags and many side streets, along with other obnoxious obstacles like rivers, parks and military bases, it's just a process of trial and error. As with bike paths, do some research in advance, get maps, use your smart phone, talk to locals — whatever you need to do.

State and National Highways

Get ready for lots of traffic, but it's rare when they don't have adequate shoulders. (The exception is when they run into cities. See above.) If you stick to paved roads, you'll find yourself on a lot of these.

Interstate Highways

Most people think riding on the interstate is cycling's answer to Russian roulette, but I argue that, at least in rural areas, they are one of the safest options you can take because of their huge shoulders. Plus, the exits are few and far between, so there's not much cross-traffic to worry about.

The downside of interstates: noise and debris. For whatever reason, authorities can't seem to keep up with the accumulation, so you have to keep a lookout for old bits of shredded tire, pieces of wood, wires and the ubiquitous broken bungee cords.

The other downside is that it's usually illegal. Each state has its own rules, so check first, but generally you will only be able to do this in the rural West, where the interstate is often the only road. Even in permissive states, you may be prevented from using interstates in urban areas, so keep an eye out for any relevant signs when approaching a city.

Some signs may even establish a time of day when you are or are not allowed to ride on the freeway.

For those obvious reasons, I never take an interstate as a first option, but when it's the only choice, it's the only choice. Over the last several years I've found myself doing time on I-90, I-25, I-84, I-70 and I-15, always as a connector of last resort between state and federal highways. It always feels a little bit weird — like I'm crashing a secret car club, but other than that I've never had any problems.

A Word About Shoulders, Safe Roads, and the Drivers of Cars

Newbies often think that adequate shoulders make or break a ride, or that it's possible to always have your own bike-friendly space, but the truth is more complicated. Many rural roads that get just a handful of cars per hour have no shoulder at all, and you're probably safer there than in the bike lane of a busy urban street. Some shoulders are wide enough for two bicycles riding abreast. Others are barely wide enough for one. What is safe? Nothing. Roads are not safe. They merely run the gamut between Death Trap and Acceptable Risk, arbitrary notions that vary depending on the rider's appetite and how many dependents they happen to have.

We play this game every day, even when driving. Some roads and some driving conditions are more dangerous than others, and we can't accurately predict how things will turn out. You could take that two-wheel drive Civic down an interstate highway covered in black ice in the middle of the night without lights and be fine. You could also get killed while driving to your neighborhood library at 20 mph at noon on a sunny day. That's life.

Here's something that is less subjective: If you limit yourself to riding on roads with generous shoulders, the world just got smaller for you. Bike tourists, much like anyone else driving a car or walking somewhere, must count on their fellow travelers to pay attention and not do anything stupid. These fellow travelers have every incentive in the world to behave themselves: They don't want to deal with the risk of personal injury, the paperwork, or the guilty conscience. Most cars will give you as wide a berth as they can.

My strategy for getting home in one piece is this: Limit yourself to riding on roads toward the "acceptable risk" side of the spectrum, ride in a predictable and sane way, wear reflective clothing, don't ride in conditions where it's tough to see cyclists, wear a helmet, keep some emergency contact information in your wallet, and after you've done all that, stop worrying about it.

Or rather, worry about something else: While getting hit by a car is not common, I've heard many stories about health problems due to heatstroke or lack of water. Friends have been laid up for days because of excessive heat, especially in areas where humidity hinders sweating. I know of one person who suffered permanent brain damage in similar circumstances. And I myself have lost a day to dehydration and another day recovering from pain due to riding in old, worn out shoes. Often, it's the less obvious stuff *that you can actually control* that will get you first.

MAPS

Maps are important. You're probably going to need some. But which kind is best?

Smart Phone Maps

Take your favorite online mapping program with you and have it show you the way.

Advantages: You get as much detail as you want, plus precise mileages if you're into that sort of thing.

Disadvantages: There is no cell service in some of America's most scenic areas, so you may need to figure out how to download your map to your phone if you want steady access. Also, keeping the phone powered will involve frequent scouting trips for outlets (Think gas stations, campgrounds) or expensive solar or dynamo gadgets.

Bike Specific Maps

Bicyclists have some unique interests: Things like the location of the next bike shop, how to get to that scenic alternate route, the elevation gain on the next hill, and where a guy can find a shower around this piece. While some organizations and governments publish a good map here and there (The State of Oregon does a great coastal route map, for example), the Adventure Cycling Association (www.adventurecycling.org) is the big tuna in this game, and their maps detail pretty much everything you would want to know.

Advantages: Better intelligence about the road ahead means less time spent talking to locals who may or may not have a good idea of what is possible or advisable on a bike.

Disadvantages: This good information doesn't come cheap, the routes offered may not go where you want to go, and talking to locals can be half the fun of a good ride.

Conventional Road Maps

This simple and elegant option is what I end up using most of the time. Get a good state or regional map from a gas station (usually between three and five bucks) and hit the road.

Advantages: They're so cheap that you can buy them, beat them up, write all over them, have locals write all over them, use them to the edge of their lives, then use them to start a campfire when you get to a new state. You can spread them out to an area much bigger than a smart phone screen, and the batteries never die. They often still work after a rainstorm.

Disadvantages: You must talk to locals to fill in the gaps, and the level of detail is not always great, especially in big cities.

Advanced Maps

Online mapping programs and road maps will be good enough for most, but if excruciating detail is your bag, fear not. If a government agency such as the Bureau of Land Management or the Forest Service manages a piece of land, they probably have a highly detailed map of it for sale. Finding it could involve a few phone calls, but it should be possible. Another good resource is any supply store that caters to professional surveyors. The one here in Albuquerque, called Holmans, is a veritable wonderland of maps, with a few wooden stakes, machetes, and sun hats thrown in for good measure. I pretty much want to move into that store.

The Interwebs

Online mapping services from Google, Bing, or Mapquest can be very handy when dreaming up routes and generally killing time while appearing to do actual work. As of this writing, Google appears to be alone in offering a mapping option tailored to bikes. This can be a great tool for mapping rural areas or short hops in cities, but when trying to navigate large metro areas I've had the hamsters inside the computer return with directions involving over 100 steps, which is a little too much help to be helpful. And it can send you down unpaved roads, so exercise caution.

If none of these options satisfy you, it never hurts to plug "bicycle routes," "bicycle route planner," or "bicycle touring [name of your state]" into your favorite search engine and see what pops up. Some websites allow you to submit your own ride to share with the universe, or you may be able to piggyback off of someone else's primo idea. Other sites are region specific and might help you get through a particular urban area. Still other sites are operated by local touring societies, which can point you to organized rides or tour routes you can do yourself. Poke around, be curious, and you'll probably hit pay dirt.

GENERAL TIPS FOR ROUTE PLANNING

Maps and roads are important, but when planning a route you also have to think about yourself. Where will I next be able to replenish my food supply? Where will I be able to sleep? Do I trust the information on the map, or the information from the man on the street I just spoke with? Do I have the energy/food to get there from here? And what would I like to see along the way?

Here's another important question, especially if you are traveling alone: When is the next time I will see a familiar face and am I okay with that? I find I can usually go one week before my own company and that of grocery store clerks wears a little thin. If you have friends along the way, be sure to stop by.

Answer these questions well, plan accordingly, and you'll probably have a safe and enjoyable ride.

WHAT TO BRING

AS WITH CONVENTIONAL TRIPS, there's really no one magic list of things to bring: Just a few guidelines. Some people pack light, some people don't care. Some people want to bring their three pound camera, but I will grow a beard to save the weight of a shaver. It's a matter of personal style. Nonetheless, I gotta tell you *something* about what to bring, so here's a list, in alphabetical order, of stuff I took on my last trip, plus a couple other obvious things that might work for you.

Audio player

I carry an mp3/FM radio player stocked to the gills with books on tape and a few Johnny Cash tunes. Mine also conveniently takes batteries, so I don't have to find a USB port to charge it (though there are plug-in USB chargers). Some kind of radio can help pass the time and might also be helpful in the event of an emergency. Should you listen to an audio player while riding? Probably not, since hearing traffic can be as important as seeing traffic. Do I do it anyway? Yes, but only in the right ear.

Bike Water Bottles

I generally travel with two. You can buy them, and the holders that either screw into or strap to your frame, at bike shops or major big box stores.

Bungee Cords

For tying down your stuff, but also for rigging up a clothesline.

Cable ('Zip') Ties

You never know when or how these things may come in handy. Bring a few and hopefully you'll never have to find out.

Chapstick

A good idea, especially in dry climates. Can double as spot hand lotion in a pinch.

Clothes

Usually two sets of clothes, one for riding and one for camp, will suffice. Since I generally ride in the summer, I wear a pair of shorts and a reflective jersey for the ride, then in the evening change into light exercise pants and a tee-shirt. For warmth I have a fleece top (that also doubles as a pillow) and a beanie. Throw in two pairs of socks and underwear and you should be fine. If you're biking in something more than easy summer weather, see "Extreme Weather Clothing." And if you are wondering how to wash all this clothing, see "Laundry Stuff."

Duct Tape

As Garrison Keillor says, it's one thing that really works. Wrap a little around a broken-off piece of pencil if you don't want to take a whole roll.

Electrical Tape

This works well for keeping food packages closed, or keeping your handlebar wrap in place. Plus, if someone asks you to wire their house, you'll be ahead of the game.

Electrolytes

You may never need to go out of your way to replenish your electrolytes, depending on where you tour. If you are seized with the urge to do so, Gatorade is easy enough to find. But if you know you will need a consistent supply, Gatorade and associated knockoffs come in cheaper powder form as well. Or you can get Tang, which is even cheaper and hearkens back to an era of American greatness. Thanks, John Glenn!

Extreme Weather Clothing

It's important to know your climate and plan appropriately. If you're biking in cold or rainy parts of the country or of the year, then sporting goods stores would be happy to sell you appropriate clothing for the task, from moisture wicking tops to neoprene booties. I solve this problem by biking mostly in dry parts of the country during dry parts of the year. When I get rained on, I get rained on, but it's not a frequent occurrence. If the weather gets truly crazy, I'll be watching it out the window of my motel room. Seriously, I can't think of a better use of money.

First Aid

For me, this means a couple of Band-Aids and a tube of Neosporin. For you, who knows?

Food

I try to carry at least a day's supply just in case I have to stop in my tracks and survive for a while. I've been carrying around the same two Power Bars for years with this contingency in mind. Beyond that, check out the chapter on eating on page 64.

Gloves

Biking gloves help protect your hands from wear and tear, while, ideally, providing padding. I've used them on most, but not all, trips. You may like them or you may not. Available at sporting goods stores.

Handkerchief

Besides the obvious use, you can tie it up around your head to absorb salty, stinging sweat before it streams into your eyes.

Headlamp

Seeing in the dark is important, and it may as well be a hands free experience. These can be had at outdoor stores, but cheaper models can sometimes be found at hardware or automotive stores, since tradesmen and DIY types use them all the time.

Hydration Packs

These are combination water bottle/backpacks. Camelbak is probably the most popular brand. I haven't needed them in the more humid parts of the country, since there is plenty of water from streams and rivers (see "Water Filtration"), and since more people live there and can support frequent gas stations. But west of the Rockies and east of the Cascades, your next water stop might be 50 miles away, and a hydration pack becomes essential. Don't mess around with the western deserts.

Insect repellent

The worse it is for you and the environment, the better it works.

Laundry

The Problem: You're carrying very few pieces of clothing and covering them with sweat and dirt on a daily basis. Solution One: Do nothing. You may stink, but you won't die. Solution Two: Find a washing machine every few days. Not easy, not cheap, but probably doable in most parts of the country. Solution Three: Carry around a small container of easily dissolved powdered laundry soap and a large Ziploc bag. Throw your clothes and some soap in the bag, fill it with water, and slosh it around for a while. To rinse, repeat process without soap as many times as needed. Hang them up to dry on a bungee cord clothesline. It's not exactly room service at the Hilton, but it'll keep the stink at bay.

Lighter

Campfires are difficult to pull off on road tours, since you can't haul much and your ability to get to the middle of a deserted area with firewood lying around is limited. But if the stars align, or if you are mountain bike touring on Forest Service roads, a lighter and a few pages from the notebook could just make your evening.

Lights

I generally don't take bike lights on tour because riding strange roads in the dark is asking for it, even with lights. On the other hand, there's always the chance you will need them. Use your good judgment. You could always use your headlamp in a pinch.

Lock

Bulletproof u-locks are not popular with the touring crowd because they weigh too much and are bulky. You could probably get away with nothing by simply keeping an eye on your bike at all times and, when this is impractical, trusting your bike to the universe and the lower crime rates of rural areas. That's my strategy on tours with garage sale bikes. Now that I have a bike worth stealing, I compromise with a coil cable lock. This keeps honest people honest and helps me enjoy the experience of grocery shopping away from my bike.

Maps

Stick 'em in a Ziploc bag and you're good to go.

Mess kit

This could be as simple as a Tupperware container and spoon. (Or even nothing — just go to McDonalds.) But if you're a little more discerning, you may want a cook stove, pot, pan, or tin plate. Outdoor supply stores will be happy to hook you up. Or, you can do what I do and survive off cold or prepared food. That saves weight, but it's more expensive and less delicious.

Mosquito Net

Probably not necessary if you have a tent, and possibly not necessary at all, depending on the time of year you travel and the particular part of the country. Still, for the sleep-under-the-stars crowd, it only takes one mosquito to ruin a good night's sleep, and it only takes one mosquito net to stop it. Look for them at sporting goods stores or find a fabric store and make your own.

Notebook

Write letters, make lists, and, in a pinch, start campfires. I also keep trip journals for posterity's sake. Do I need to remind you to bring a pen here? Why not...

Plastic Bags

Just about everything I take is packed into a Ziploc bag for the sake of organization and waterproofness. Throw in a few extra just in case. Plastic grocery bags could also come in real handy along the way, so keep a couple on hand.

Phone

Turns out texting your location once a day is a fun way to impress your friends. Talking to people is also a good way to get information and stay sane. (More in "How to Ride," page 48.) For those who are anti-phone except in emergencies, know that old, decommissioned cell phones will usually still call 911 (check with the phone company). Put the word out and you can probably find one. Other companies sell 911-only phones.

Reading Material

Cheap paperbacks, magazines, and newspapers are especially good for the road, since whatever you bring is likely to get pretty beat up. Leave that first edition Gutenberg Bible at home. Smart phone reading apps are good for this as well, assuming you don't mind hunting down electrical outlets all the time or springing for a solar or dynamo charger (Google it).

Reflective Gear

See and be seen is not just a motto for New York socialites. When making decisions about clothing, save a special place in your heart for light colors. Think about getting a few reflectors for the spokes of your wheels. Reflective jackets are a good way to be seen as well, though you can save money by using the sort of reflective vest that construction workers wear. You can find these at hardware stores, home improvement stores, and any supply house frequented by tradesmen.

Soap

I just carry around one bar and use it in lieu of shampoo as well. Those who actually want to take care of their hair should probably find travel sized bottles of shampoo, etc.

Shoes

A light pair of sandals or sneakers may be just the ticket to supplement whatever you wear when riding.

Shorts, Cycling

If you bring only one crazy Lycraesque garment, it should be cycling shorts. Because of special padding and strategically placed seams, cycling shorts are designed to make you look like a deranged competitor in some medieval battle staged in a park by the Society for Creative Anachronism. No. Sorry. That just came out. They are designed to reduce chafing, which can be very painful. Available at sporting goods stores and, of course, online. I have not needed them so far. Why? I have no idea, though I do consider this to be strong evidence for the existence of God.

Sleeping equipment

Tents are the obvious choice for shelter, but the disadvantage is that they are either expensive and light, or cheap and heavy. I generally sleep under the stars and rig up a tarp shelter between a couple of nearby trees in case of rain. Tarps vary from the $5 kind you get at home improvement stores to fancier light ones, designed for camping, that come with stakes and tie straps. Another idea is to use a bivy sack, which can only be described as a large condom for your sleeping bag. (Google it and tell me I'm wrong.) Either way, rig things up so that it shelters you and doesn't blow away.

You'll probably need a sleeping bag and some sort of pad as well. Sleeping bags can be bulky or compact, designed for warm or cold weather. Pads vary in size, comfort, and price. Do some research to figure out what's best for your particular packing arrangement and wallet. I have a Thermarest air mattress and 30 degree sleeping bag, and both have served me well for many years.

Whatever you do, don't test out your equipment on a bike ride. First use it a couple of times car camping or in your backyard.

Sunglasses

If you don't need sunglasses on a trip, I suspect it will be a very sad trip. But if cloudy days and/or rain are more than a possibility, consider bringing cloud-friendly eye protection. Outdoor stores will happily cater to your every whim in this department, but if you want to save a few bucks buy a pair of safety glasses or goggles from a hardware or home improvement store instead. At five bucks or so, you'll feel better about life when they inevitably get lost or scratched up. In any event, squinting while your face gets pelted with rain gets old fast.

Sunscreen

Skin cancer = bad.

Tire, Tube, Pump and Patch Kit

...and know how to use them (watch a youtube video or ask a friend). Hand pumps are not created equal, by the way. Some can barely put 60 pounds of pressure into a tire, which is enough for many mountain bike tires but not road tires, which generally take between 90 and 110 pounds. Of course, that kind of pressure doesn't come cheap in a hand pump.

If you don't want to spring for a good pump, you can probably limp along at low pressure, though this increases the chances of flats. You can borrow pumps from bike shops or random strangers. Or, if you are using schrader valve tubes, you can try this dirtbag solution: Use your lousy pump to inflate the tire as much as you can, then ride to a truck stop or gas station and top it off with their compressor (about $1 these days, but sometimes free). Carry a tire gauge so you can tell how much pressure you've added. Watch out for overinflated tires. They are no fun, unless of course you enjoy hearing sounds that make you wonder if you're being shot at.

Also watch to make sure you get the right kind of compressor pump: Car tires don't need the pressure that road bike tires require, but tuck tires do. Not all compressors are created equal.

Toilet Kit

Between gas stations, restaurants, parks and campgrounds this may very well go unused throughout your trip. But for those times when nature won't take "wait a minute" for an answer, it's good to have access to some toilet paper and a mini bottle of hand sanitizer. Toilet paper can also take the form of a bunch of folded paper napkins or a miniature packet of tissues. These are less likely to end up as an unrecognizable wads of lint. Hand sanitizer is especially convenient in rural areas, where outhouses are more common.

Tools

Some kind of multi-tool or Swiss army knife will come in handy when cutting up food, opening cans, or when working on anything bike related that requires a screw driver. You can also pick up a cheap hex wrench set from a hardware store and carry with you only those wrenches that will tighten parts of your particular bike. Jerry the Bike Mechanic also recommends the Alien Tool by Topeak. It's pretty much a bike shop in five cubic inches. For more on this, see "Troubleshooting" on page 70.

Tooth Cleaning and Other Personal Toiletries

Often such items as toothpaste come in smaller travel sizes. This is an easy way to cut down on weight. And if you want to sound particularly hardcore when explaining this to your friends, tell them you saw your toothbrush in half to save a few precious ounces. Whether you actually do this or not is up to you.

Towel

A bath towel is probably too bulky, but a hand towel works well as a miniature replacement, post shower.

Water Filtration

Along more populated routes, a water filter may not be strictly necessary. Still, you may want one anyway because it increases your camping options. My filter has more than paid for itself by allowing me to camp for free beside, say, some scenic river, rather than paying for a campsite. One compromise is to bring a bottle of water purification tablets. In a pinch, these will make water from streams safe to drink, but don't count on good taste. Note: there are many details of water purification I've left out because they are specific to your ride or your purification method. Do your research, read the labels, and try not to poison yourself.

HOW TO RIDE

RIDING A LONG DISTANCE is a chameleonesque exercise in adaptation. Every day will bring a new situation, a new set of challenges. Sometimes, the challenge (a cattle guard, for instance) is a routine you can conquer with a formulaic solution. I've tried to list as many of those as I can below, though rest assured, you will end up blazing a new troubleshooting trail at some point.

The biggest challenges, however, arise from your own mind. I'm confident that tens of millions of Americans are physically capable of riding a bike for a long distance. But only a small fraction of those people are psychologically capable, because the stakes can seem so overwhelming. Shock, fear, and avoidance are perfectly natural reactions to the idea of riding to the next state over.

But if you get yourself comfortable enough to ride, a whole new set of issues emerges as you surrender to the road and the weather. One day, Mother Nature may decide to rain on you. She may provide you with a long series of rolling hills, one of the most maddening topographies out there. One day, you will surely come across the Touring Trifecta: Uphill, headwind, in the rain. On the flip side, you may get the wind at your back and some awesome scenery to boot.

You can get all the tricked out clothing and energy bars that your bank account will support. It barely matters. Bicycle touring is often a process of sucking it up and dealing. It's about learning to enjoy yourself in adverse conditions, because the weather is rarely perfect, and then, not for long. You will learn to adapt, to thrive under whatever sky you find yourself, or your first ride will be your last.

A tour is an incredibly stressful experience in the sense that it takes us outside the routines of normal life. Instead of a house, you have a sleeping bag and a patch of grass or, at best, a motel. Instead of a climate controlled car, you have some clothes and, hopefully, the ability to brush off a little discomforting rain. You sleep in a different place every night, meet new people every day, and often eat strange food.

Taking yourself out of your protective cocoon, enlisting your muscles in a battle with the elements and the little ribbon of road stretching into the distance — It's the stuff of epic myth. It clears the mind, invades your dreams, and heightens your emotions.

On the good days, I begin to understand what Winston Churchill must have felt like when he accepted the unconditional surrender of the Third Reich. On the bad days, I think of Job and marvel at all we have in common. The first couple of days, with the stress of readjustment, are usually the hardest. This situation is probably made worse by my general insistence on traveling alone.

Learning to navigate these psychological hills and valleys is not just a good skill to help you on your trip. It's a good skill that will help you with the rest of your life. It lends calming perspective to the normal interpersonal and professional bumps that anyone with a job, a significant other, or, for that matter, a pulse, is going to run into. This too shall pass, grasshopper, just like that hill from hell on the last trip.

As with many challenges, the trick here is to roll with it. Let your mind wander. Talk to yourself. Talk to livestock. Scream. Yell. Go on a vision quest. Do whatever you have to do to ride the wave. Think of a bike trip as a kind of alternate universe, like camp or Las Vegas. You are alone in the middle of nowhere, and the typical rules of polite society don't really apply to you.

PRACTICAL TIPS & COMMON OBSTACLES
Know Things

Always have in mind the next place you are going to get food and water, and a couple of ideas on where you are going to sleep that night. No one ever lay on their deathbed regretting having made excessive backup plans. You can get this information from maps and Internet research, but published information is not always accurate or up-to-date. For the latest, ask people. Gas station attendants, welcome center desk jockeys, and people wandering around on the street can probably help, but beware of their car-oriented world view: They cannot always be trusted to distinguish between a mere gas station and a gas station with attached convenience store. I've even run into people who sent me down an unpaved road they thought was paved, and people who see no difference between five and twenty miles.

Beware of Wind

Adjusting your riding style to the wind — whatever direction it's coming from — is easy enough, but when going down hills at high speeds be ready for crazy cross breezes to pop out from behind a bend without much warning. This is especially true when emerging from protective road cuts. Wind can blow you right off the road or into traffic if you're not careful.

Passing Cars

Especially on long country roads where you will probably spend most of your time, an overwhelming majority of cars will pass you with no trouble at all, going well into the other lane if need be. But trouble crops up when there is already a car in the other lane traveling in the opposite direction, and this is when you get the exhilarating experience of having a car pass you at close range at upwards of 50 miles per hour. More rarely, you will be on the other side of this situation: A car in the opposite lane will pass another car in the opposite lane, and you will come face-to-face with that car, going highway speed plus the ten miles per hour you add to the equation. (I'm confident that if Dante had been a bicycle tourist, he would have noted a special circle in hell for these people.) In either situation, it's important that you stay predictable. Don't do anything that would distract the drivers from their delicate maneuvers. If you have room to work with on the side of the road, move over. If not, remember that this situation generally is less dangerous than it feels.

Also keep in mind: Vehicles with a large mass will create their own wind. Usually this comes in the form of a tail wind whoosh as they pass. It shouldn't drive you off the road, but you should be aware of it.

Riding in the Dark

This is not recommended. It can be done, but you are more likely to run into stuff and injure yourself or your bike, especially since you don't know the road very well. If you choose to do it anyway, deploy a full court press of lights and reflective gear.

Bridges

Even if the road has a generous shoulder, the bridge may not. Approach these on a case-by-case basis. Sometimes I will stop and wait for a lull in the traffic before proceeding. Other times I have walked my bike over a bridge, using a sidewalk too narrow for riding. In a few rare cases, I have taken over the center of the lane, a brash and nerve racking move that nonetheless forces cars to find another lane or sit and wait for you to safely get to the other side. They may not like it, but it's better than getting wedged into a concrete barrier. This strategy can be used on narrow roads of all kinds, especially in downtown core areas.

Tunnels

The same shoulder issues that bridges bring also come standard in tunnels, and the same remedies can apply. But three things make tunnels different: First, sound is magnified and this can be very disconcerting if a car enters the tunnel behind you. Second, at the entrance to some tunnels, you can press a button that lights up a handy "Bicycle in Tunnel" display that — hopefully — cars will pay attention to. Third, tunnels are sometimes very dark. If called for, treat it like riding at night.

Cattle Guards

A series of metal rails spaced a couple of inches apart, you can technically ride over these but I don't recommend it. Especially with thin tires, you'll find that the effect is similar to someone hitting your back with the bottom sides of their fists, except you feel it in a slightly more sensitive region. Walking my bike over sounds much easier, thanks, especially considering that many are poorly maintained and feature dangerous gaps. You will find that, tragically enough, many of these guards are located at the bottom of hills, a popular point for delineating property lines. This means you may have to stop very fast to avoid them. But if you look up and realize it's too late, just make the motor boat hum and try to enjoy yourself as much as you can.

Trucks and Over-sized Loads

The only time I've run myself off the road intentionally was to escape an over-sized load, usually part of a house. But two things work in your favor with these giants of the highway: First, warning cars with flashing lights usually act as escort, so you get a little advanced warning. Second, commercially licensed truck drivers are much better drivers than your average civilian. If you want something to fear, think about that 75-year-old retired tax attorney at the helm of his new Greyhound-bus-sized RV. That rig, ladies and gentlemen, *does not require any special training or license*. Stay alert.

Construction Projects

Especially in the summer construction season, you will no doubt run into a few whoppers. Your best bet is to ride to the head of the line and ask the flagger or some other official what to do. Most crews will have some experience dealing with cyclists, but they use different strategies for getting them through safely. Sometimes they have told me to ride along with the cars, other times they have held up all traffic, giving me the whole road. Sometimes I have been given a mere head start. And once, in Utah, they told me to throw my bike in the pilot car (usually a truck, ironically enough) and ride through on official escort.

LODGING

THIS IDEA OF SLEEPING IN A NEW PLACE every night, often on the ground, can be intimidating for the uninitiated, or for those who have endured a few sleepless nights in a strange campground somewhere. But touring is different because there's nothing quite like an enormous amount of exercise to help you sleep. No matter how accustomed you are to creature comforts, you will get used to camping. It wasn't too long ago that pretty much all humans were camping every night, after all, and our physiology hasn't changed that much since. Still, if that's a bridge too far, leave the camping gear at home and stay in motels.

Whatever your feelings on this issue, options abound. Here they are, in descending order of luxury.

Hotels and motels

Beds really are wonderful things when you get right down to it, and I've never found a hotel or motel that didn't have one. They offer the best security out there — just wheel the bike right into your room. They are often located near sources of food and entertainment. And you can watch all the TV you want. My not-so-secret ambition is to stay in them exclusively.

Still, all the TV you want might keep you up too late, burning prime sleeping time and giving you a later start the next day. Plus, hotels and motels are expensive. Did you really set out to bike some jaw-dropping distance because you can't live without a few creature comforts? We didn't think so.

Hostels

They're usually cheap enough and full of interesting fellow travelers, especially western Europeans on their government-mandated 46 weeks of annual vacation. They're probably going to be more receptive to quirky bike tourists than a motel. Plus, with common areas and dorm-style sleeping arrangements, hostels are architecturally well equipped to inspire conversations with others.

Still, hostels are few and far between, and often located in urban jungles. (Ask yourself: Would a German engineering student care to visit Driggs, Idaho?) Dorm-style sleeping arrangements mean you should bring ear plugs for the inevitable snoring. And some are dens of thieves.

Informal Places Found on the Web

If you're looking to stay indoors but not spend too much look no further than the internet. Sites like couchsurfing.org will let you crash with complete strangers, all for the low, low price of agreeing to host others. The site warmshowers.org even caters specifically to bicycle tourists. For a more complete list of similar sites, plug "Wikitravel Hospitality Exchange" into your favorite search engine.

One-night rentals can also be found at airbnb.com. Some folks use this site to rent out their extra mansion, and you'll pay dearly for that. Others just rent out a room and a bed, and some good deals can be had for the spartan traveler. Airbnb is the big dog in this market, but serious competitors are bound to pop up too.

Sleeping indoors could be advantage enough, but there are two reasons for caution: Some of these sites may require a fair amount of planning in advance, and that's always difficult on a bike trip. Also, many people sign up for hospitality exchanges like Couchsurfing because they want to meet and talk to new people. If that's why you're on a bike trip too, this could be a match made in heaven, but introvert loners take note.

One more FYI: These opportunities are, as you would expect, generally confined to population centers.

RV Parks

You might think that RV parks are for, well, RVs, but many if not most also feature tent sites, usually for $10-20. A few that don't have such sites may let you camp on a patch of grass anyway. They are pretty informal places.

This is by far my favorite category of lodging. I've never found one that didn't have a shower, and most are very well kept up, catering as they must to the affluent retired set. Laundry services come standard as well. Finding an electrical outlet is a snap. They are more likely to be located within striking distance of urban amenities. And I've never felt safer as a bicyclist. Elderly Republicans simply aren't after your expensive pump. The only downside is the cost: It's about as expensive as camping gets.

RV Parks are also great because they usually provide options for what exactly you can sleep on. They often have grass, but also picnic tables. For those of us who prefer sleeping under the stars, picnic tables are a great platform: they're level, clean, and they reduce the odds of a nose-to-nose encounter with a skunk or other fauna.

Mobile Home Parks

Located on the other side of the tracks from the RV parks, these can still be decent enough places to crash for the night. Cheap too. But don't count on there being toilet paper in the bathroom. Sleeping arrangements could be very ad hoc as well, but find the manager and see what you can negotiate. And while I've never had a bad experience with the clientele, elderly Republicans they ain't.

State and Local Parks

They are generally pleasant places and often have those all-important showers (But be prepared with quarters). They are often reasonably priced. The better campgrounds feature primitive campsites, sometimes called hiker/biker sites. You will probably get a picnic table and a patch of grass and not much else, but the price is usually much lower than a formal car camping site. But hit the wrong one and watch out: You'll pay a price better suited to a family of six with two cars. Another disadvantage: The actual families of six at the park might make a lot of noise.

National Parks

Here you can revel in the grand sight of our nation's scenic treasures. Unfortunately, it's possible that the rest of the country had the same idea and caused a traffic jam, if you're at a more iconic park (if not, you may practically have the place to yourself). Showers may be hard to come by. Entrance fees are common.

National Forest, Bureau of Land Management, and other Federal Campgrounds

Here you can revel in the grand sight of our nation's scenic treasures that didn't have the rotten luck of being classified as a national park. They're often cheap, especially if they don't have running water or electricity. Nearby creeks or rivers can pinch hit for a real shower, but the real hot water deal will be hard to find. A word of warning: Some are actually quite expensive for no apparent reason.

Dispersed Camping on Federal Lands

This is a great option to those comfortable camping without toilets or picnic tables. Be sure to check local conditions for exceptions, but in general it's okay to camp anywhere on BLM or national forest land provided you dispose of waste properly, obey fire regulations, and don't set up too close to a waterway. Both the BLM and the Forest Service publish additional guidelines for dispersed camping on the web, and they are worth reviewing.

On the plus side, there are no camping fees and usually no neighbors. But often the best dispersed campsites are hard to reach on a bike.

Non-traditional authorized camping

Put this one in the "it never hurts to ask" file: If you come to a town and there's no obvious campground, just start asking around. Odds are pretty good you'll find a patch of grass behind a gas station, a church yard, a church proper, somebody's front lawn, or a cemetery that some authority figure — be they duly sworn or more on the informal side — will allow you to camp in. You might even get invited into the spare room of a house. Provisions for water and bathrooms are negotiable. This option is ideal for outgoing charismatic types who are not afraid to ask for stuff.

Non-traditional unauthorized camping

Many bike tourists, being well accustomed to breaking social norms, will camp in any old place without asking: the aforementioned cemetery or field, some abandoned building, the side of the road behind a couple of trees, a rest stop, beside those piles of gravel that road crews stash at random places, etc. It's quite possible, especially in rural areas, that you will get away with this 99 times out of 100. Even if you are spotted, most people either don't care or don't want to bother doing anything about it.

While it is free, the disadvantages are thus: Because this often amounts to illegal trespassing, you may need to hide yourself well, and this complicates supply and bathroom runs. Successful stealth campers will set up camp when darkness is near and be gone first thing in the morning, taking care to cover up any reflective material that may give away their position during the night.

Even if you make no effort to hide, you will probably get away with camping at the entrance to that church or the gazebo in the town square. It all depends on what kind of mood the landowners, cops, and passersby happen to be in. (Personally, shelling out a few bucks for the official legitimacy of a campsite seems like a small price to pay for the privilege of avoiding middle-of-the-night diplomacy with a cop's flashlight in one's face, but maybe I'm just a hopeless square here.)

EATING

IN NORMAL LIFE, WE EAT. On bike trips, we feed. This is not good natured dining as an accessory to enjoying good company, tasting new treats, and generally living the good, civilized life. This is the quick, dirty, and efficient conveyance of calories into your body.

This thought occurred to me on tour last year as I finished eating a jar of peanut butter with a spoon (in the back parking lot of a suburban Salt Lake gas station, no less), and realized that not one bit of this food substance had, in its short life, been spread on anything before consumption. It was a feeding tube, disguised as a plastic jar.

Ladies, bike trip dining is your chance to discover what it is like to be a 14-year-old boy about to grow two inches. You may find yourself eating a big lunch, snacking all afternoon, then still hungry for dinner. Guys, you may soon find yourself sympathizing with pregnant women, attacked by sudden cravings for pickles, ice cream, and all manner of other randomness.

Your appetite will probably keep ramping up the longer you are on the road. Day two may seem pretty normal, but after ten days you may find yourself eating a rotisserie chicken, four tomatoes, and a pint of ice cream for dinner (true story). For breakfast on the last day of one trip, I ate three doughnuts and a package of mixed dried fruit, washing it down with a quart of whole milk.

If you are picky about your food, you may want to put your feelings on hold for the duration of the trip, but the biological reality of exercising all day may just take care of it for you. Eating/feeding becomes an all-day affair, something essential if you're going to keep your energy up (it's best to eat way before you hit that wall of dazed hunger). I generally stop every ten miles or every hour, whichever comes first. On those breaks, I almost always eat something.

Despite this savage gluttony, I always lose weight on trips, a nice little side benefit that I probably should have played up on the cover. Suffice it say that eating whatever you damn well please is really, really fun. Food never tasted so good.

On the road, your options for food are thus:

Restaurants

They offer (usually) delicious hot food and you don't have to prepare it. You can get your money's worth at all-you-can-eat buffets, and no cooking equipment is necessary. But some restaurants may require that you look and/or smell good, and depending on the shower situation at your camp, this could be a challenge. Also, this is the most expensive food option.

Grocery Store as Restaurant

You need not take along a camp stove to enjoy reasonably priced food, if you're willing to get along with grocery store deli fare. Combine it with the odd can of chili, quart of milk, bunch of bananas, and sandwich fixings (I use tortillas in lieu of bread for ease of transport), and you'll be set. This way, you don't have to mess with cooking or steeply priced restaurants. Still, a poorly stocked grocery store could mean you eat poorly now and then. Worse, if there is only a gas station to be found you could find yourself dining on cold Chef Boyardee ravioli with Slim Jims and a two-year-old cheese Danish for dessert (another true story). One silver lining: Rural gas stations are generally more holistically stocked than your typical urban 7-11. You might even find some sad looking produce.

Hint: Don't turn your nose up at dollar stores. They can be treasure troves of cycling friendly food.

Grocery Store as Source of Materials for Cooking

This is what sensible people do. Carry around a few pounds of rice or other grain, some fast-cooking variety of beans, then supplement it with fruits and vegetables. Seriously. One of these years I will starting doing this.

It's cheap and much healthier than the aforementioned cheese Danish. This method also results in a minimum amount of packaging being tossed into the trash. But there's a high barrier to entry: lots of little techniques to know, lots of specialty gear to research and buy, and lots of stuff to clean up afterwards. And the equipment adds weight and bulk.

Dumpster Diving

What are you, nuts?

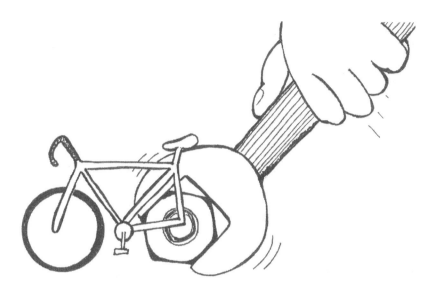

TROUBLESHOOTING

MECHANICAL DIFFICULTIES, like death and taxes, are just a part of life. Unless you are extremely lucky or your bike is built like a tank, you'll have to deal with them. But that brings up some important questions: What should you be prepared to fix? And what sorts of spare parts should you bring along?

Many bike experts and touring manual authors will now present a specific list of things to bring and repairs you should know how to do. Forget that. This is a matter of personal style, and you get to choose just how prepared you want to be. If you like repairing bikes and you're good at it, then load up a bunch of tools and hit the road. If all of your family's mechanical know-how went to your brother, you can still hit the road and probably be fine. The worst case scenario is that you'll have to stick your thumb out and meet one of the small army of American motorists who have a soft spot in their hearts for stranded bicyclists. (This may be required even without any mechanical trouble. Someone could steal your bike, you may suddenly have to get to a funeral 1,000 miles away, etc.)

Q: All well and good, but what *can* go wrong, mechanically speaking?
A: To answer that, let's look in my personal history of cycling mishaps.

2007: On the Oregon Coast, a piece of bark flies into my spokes and breaks two of them. The wheel wobbled, but I still rode it another 120 miles to a bike shop, where a perplexed mechanic fixed it. This trip also included a few flat tires, which I fixed on the spot.

2008: Near Grangeville, Idaho, a couple more spokes bite the dust. After my attempts at a hack repair make a bad situation even worse, a local family swoops in and takes me to a junkyard operated by some relation of theirs. For five dollars, I come away with a wobbly but still functional wheel that I rode for the next 300 miles to Glacier National Park.

2009: On a tour of central Colorado, I somehow manage to get half a dozen flat tires. I repair all of these on the spot.

2011: While riding in the dark less than one mile from my home in Albuquerque, I crash into a median, bending the frame beyond repair and cracking a rib. Remember when I said not to ride in the dark? Now you know why.

2011: On day one of a tour, a brake lever snaps off and the spindle that connects the pedal crankshaft starts to separate. Being so close to home, Jerry the Bike Mechanic bails me out of this one by lending me a bike that is of much higher quality. It gives me no problems at all, and despite some reservations about losing some dangerous touring flavor, I buy it off of him.

Q: So *everything* can go wrong?
A: Yes and no. In 4,000 miles of touring, I've had a few things break, but none of those things ended my trip. (The crash would have, had I been on tour.) And the separating crankshafts might have ended it, but being so close to home I didn't have to find out. Overall, not a bad track record. Also, keep in mind that I did all but the most recent tours on bikes that would have been tough to unload at a garage sale.

Q: Breaking down in central Idaho does not sound like any fun at all.
A: On one hand, you're right, and if you want nothing more than to reduce that possibility to its absolute minimum, get a high quality bike, make sure a good mechanic looks it over before you head out, and make sure you know about bike repair. On the other hand, you're wrong, because I ended up meeting some very interesting fellow Americans while breaking down in central Idaho. Looking back on that experience, it was a stressful time, but at the end of the day, just part of the adventure. Remember that the Chinese use the same character for "crisis" and "opportunity."

Q: What is the absolute minimum I should be prepared to fix?
A: You should be able to repair punctured inner tubes, replace tires, and boot tires (Youtube it). That will mean knowing the size and style of your tire well enough to pick it out on a store shelf or talk about it with a clerk. You should also know how to re-attach a chain that has fallen off or otherwise derailed. (Generally this means getting your hands very greasy — a possible reason to take along a few pairs of latex or nitrile gloves.) Another good idea is to buy a cheap hex wrench set and bring along only those wrenches that could tighten down something on your bike. I would also bring along some electrical tape, some duct tape (roll

some onto a broken pencil to save space), some bailing wire and some zip ties. And don't forget your pocket knife or multi-tool.

Q: Beyond that, what's the low hanging fruit of bike repair? In other words, what's the least amount of stuff I can learn, the smallest number of tools I can buy, while still covering as many bases as I can in the emergency repair department?

A: Jerry the Bike Mechanic recommends you know the following: (1.) How to fix a broken chain, (2.) how to replace a brake or gear shift cable, and (3.) how to replace a broken spoke. Find a good book or search it out on youtube, then carry the right replacement parts and the Alien Tool by Topeak, plus something to cut metal, like the wire cutters on a multi-tool. Between youtube, friends, and your bike mechanic, learning this stuff shouldn't be too hard.

 TIP FROM JERRY: Especially if it rains, you'll need to make sure your chain stays lubricated. You could bring a small bottle of chain lube, but this is the coward's way out. Instead, pay a visit to an auto supply store or gas station and root around in the garbage for a spent bottle of motor oil. Even though it's of no use to a motorist, the dregs of that bottle probably represent a year's supply of chain lube. Or you could buy a fresh bottle and have yourself a 50-year supply. But this is also the coward's way out.

HOW TO HITCHHIKE

When all else fails, you may find yourself doing this. Given the potential danger and the fact that police sometimes frown on the practice, I would use it only after establishing that there are no good options for public transportation available and that you cannot practically walk your way to some kind of civilization.

1. Find a place with a wide shoulder where traffic is moving as slowly as possible, such as a junction or just outside of a town before a highway gets up to full speed. Remember that you are

making a silent sales pitch, and the slower the traffic, the more precious seconds you will have to make it.

2. Flaunt your bicycling credentials. Wear your biking clothes, even if you have the option of not doing so. Wear your helmet. And if you can demonstrate visually that your bike needs repair, do so. Hitchhiking with a bike is not easy, since many potential rides do not have lots of extra space, but you can make the most of the situation by embracing your inner bicyclist. Eventually, another member of this club will take pity on you and stop. Or, someone who is desperately bored out of their skull and craving human conversation will stop. I've had both experiences.

3. Make a sign with your destination printed on it, if at all possible.

4. Look as clean cut and respectable as you can. Ask yourself if you would pick yourself up.

5. Be very careful. Trust your gut. I've never had a bad experience hitchhiking, but it is certainly a possibility, especially if you are a woman. Ask questions before getting in. Text the license plate number, make and model of the car, and a physical description and name of the driver to a friend. Accidentally drop your concealed weapons permit on the floor or mention some great gift your mom got you in honor of your making black belt. Do whatever you need to do to stay safe.

TRANSPORTING YOUR BIKE

THIS IS ALWAYS A LOGISTICAL HEADACHE, and my favorite strategy is to avoid it altogether. I generally start or end my trips in my hometown, eliminating half of the problem. (One could, of course, do a loop that starts and ends at one's house, but I have psychological issues with this. I like getting somewhere new.)

Unfortunately, there are few viable strategies to avoid taking apart your bike and putting it in a box. You could ride a complete piece of garbage and then abandon it at the end of the trip. You could also look into renting a bike, which might solve all or part of the problem. Or this slightly better option: Coordinate with your friends. If they go on a road trip, go with them and ride all the way back, or the other way around. You don't have much control over where you ride, but you do get to spend some quality time with your friends, and you'll save the hassle of shipping.

You could also drive yourself and your bike to a starting point and then make some kind of loop out of it, though finding a safe place for your car could be a challenge.

But sooner or later, you'll no doubt have to put your bike in a special (big) box and ship it somewhere. Essentially that involves taking off the wheels, the pedals, the seat, and the handle bars and carefully packing them in. There are some good YouTube videos that demonstrate how to do this if you are a do-it-yourself kind of person. Bike boxes can often be had for free or a nominal fee at bike shops. You can buy hard-shell bike shipping containers as well, though having an expensive and not-very-disposable case to deal with could present its own problems.

Bike shops will also pack up a bike for you, usually charging $30-60 for the favor. Some bike shops will even ship it for you, most likely via UPS or FedEx. That will probably be the most convenient thing for you to do, because at this point in the trip you will be a pedestrian with a huge box to carry around. It's best to plan these logistics out carefully.

This is why I try to end my trips in towns where my friends live. You certainly can end a trip in a strange town, but the process will be much easier if you have access to a car and someone who knows his or her way around. Plus, you have to visit your friends at some point, and they'll be impressed if you ride your bike.

How much will it cost? In my experience, who the hell knows? I've shipped the same bike for $35 in one instance, and $110 in another — on the same carrier no less. Little differences in weight and box size can make a big difference, it seems. Shop around if you can, but otherwise just hand over your credit card and think of England.

Here are some of your shipping options, with commentary from Jerry:

1. **FedEx Ground** — Great option. It's timely, relatively cheap, and goes everywhere. Sterling record of delivering undamaged parcels.

2. **UPS Ground** — Roughly the same timeline as FedEx, but often more expensive.

3. **United States Postal Service** — Not commonly used, but it can be competitive.

4. **Greyhound** — Can be slow and must be well packed, but could be a viable option, especially if you are traveling with the bike.

5. **Amtrak** — This is a great option if Amtrak happens to have a baggage office where you are going. Amtrak bike boxes are bigger than average, so you may just have to take the wheels off instead of a more thorough disassembly.

6. **Airlines** — This may be worth exploring if you're flying anyway, especially if you have a hard shell case that can withstand weight being placed on top of it. Expect to pay a significant fee, and expect the rules to change frequently.

BIKE PEOPLE

WHO ARE THESE PEOPLE? Really, what kind of a person does this sort of thing? The answer: You, I hope. You got this far, after all, so it's high time you joined the ranks.

But to actually answer the question, yes, some demographic trends do emerge after you've been on the road long enough. Generally, bike tourists fit into five categories:

1. **Young Guns**: Students, interns, newlyweds, and others whose career commitments are measured in months, rather than years, and who often find themselves with summers to kill or time between jobs.

2. **Cool Old People**: Still active and now with loads of free time.

3. **The Restless**: Fed up with their careers, their marriages, the military industrial complex, or their lives in general, they seek a moment or two of transcendence, hoping the open road will show them their next move.

4. **Dirtbags**: They get food and tires from dumpsters and never pay for campsites.

5. **Wildcards**: Here we have everyone else. Some just get away for a week or two when they can. Others are in it to obsess about how much mileage they can cover. Still others take their laptops and continue working from motels while on the road. You never know. The normal people alluded to in this book's subtitle also fit in here. Here's hoping there will be more of them soon.

In any event, they're an interesting bunch. Let's meet a few.

Name: *Minnie McMahon*

Age: *28*

Home base: *Pescadero, CA*

Touring history: *Cambridge, MA-Halifax, Nova Scotia; Portland, OR-Los Angeles; loop of Long Island, NY; loop of Death Valley, CA.; weekend trips around the San Joaquin Delta, Massachusetts, and San Francisco Bay Area.*

Memorable touring experience: *Traveling with a group, she got lost in Death Valley and ended up*  *getting rescued by a group of guys from Las Vegas and their six Jeeps. While visiting the group's cabin, the cyclists learned that it was the very place where, in 1969, authorities had finally arrested the serial killer Charles Manson.*

Hot Tip for a Smooth Trip: *One great way to orient yourself to a new location is by sampling the local ice cream.*

A GROUP OF CHILDHOOD FRIENDS first hatched the idea of riding across the country, but Minnie McMahon was not a fan. That brand of outrageous adventure — it was just not something she did.

But after a little introspection (and maybe peer pressure), she started to have second thoughts.

"Why don't I decide that it's something I do?" she asked herself.

Why not, indeed.

A poorly timed illness nixed the cross-country trip, but later that summer she and a friend rode north along the coast of Maine instead, taking a ferry to Canada and continuing on to Halifax. And just like that, a skeptic was hooked on touring.

"You just feel so good. It's like no other thing. It's freedom," McMahon says. "It's so cliché but your presence in the moment is much more easily felt and experienced."

If touring can border on the spiritual, McMahon has also enjoyed some practical benefits. On tour in California one day, she happened to spend an afternoon with Daniel Kim, who at the time was her sister's roommate. They kept in touch, and later that year went out on a date.

A really long date.

They rode from Cambridge, Massachusetts to Long Island, where they ran into Hurricane Earl and had to take shelter with family friends.

The two remain a couple to this day, but there's no word on where they went for their second date.

McMahon is unusual in that she has often travels with groups of women. Anecdotal evidence suggests that while co-ed groups are common, all-female groups are not, and solo female riders even less so. While that may be due to perceptions of safety, McMahon says the rules of everyday life apply to touring as well.

"You're going to follow your gut as to what feels okay, and maybe fewer places feel okay for women," she says. "That's just what you have to do on a bike tour, too. You do have to be careful but you don't have to be more careful than normal life."

Name: *Ed Gross*
Age: *77*
Homebase: *Brookings, OR*
Touring history: *El Paso-St. Paul; Spokane-St. Paul; Eastern Nevada to San Francisco, then up the coast to just over the Oregon border.*
Memorable touring experience: *When inquiring at a small-town tavern about spending the night in a city park across the street, Gross got recruited to serve as official photographer for a 25th wedding anniversary party at the tavern.*
Hot Tip for a Smooth Trip: *Be very careful when riding in high heat in humid areas because sweating only cools the body if evaporation is possible. Once when touring through Iowa, a case of heat exhaustion took him out of action for two days.*

SOMETIMES ALL YOU NEED TO MOTIVATE YOURSELF to take a tour is a serious injury — say, snapping a critical tendon in your left foot during a disagreement with a tree planting tool. That's what happened to Ed Gross, a retired U.S. Forest Service soil scientist from Brookings, Oregon, back in 1996.

"It was hell," he says.

Gross found himself stuck at home in a cast for a month, reading "Over the Hills," a touring travelogue by David Lamb, thinking, "this if for me!"

No stranger to two-wheeled transport, Gross is a lifelong bike commuter, wherever his studies or career have taken him.

"I've had bikes stolen in all kinds of nice places," he says. "I get a high every day I'm riding my bike. It's that endorphin stuff. Makes you feel really good and increases thinking power. Ideas are a dime a dozen as the endorphins flow."

Following a career spent outdoors with the Forest Service, he adapted quickly to the free and easy style of solo cross-country travel. An experienced camper, he slept in whatever country church yard, arroyo or highway culvert he happened upon. But while others tour to see America, or restore their faith in the American people, Gross is in it for the science. In much the same way that contractors will evaluate every building they enter with a knowing and appreciative eye, he enjoys taking in America's streams, rocks, soils and plants. His trip journals are full of observations concerning the water levels of lakes, the smell of rotting algae, and the prevalence of local wildlife.

"Just seeing the different countrysides. You get to see everything up close. It's really a thrill. I generally avoid — if I can — cities."

Name: *Stephen Gillan*
Age: *34*
Homebase: *Fort Collins, CO*
Touring history: *A.C.A. transcontinental route, southern tier; A.C.A. continental divide route.*

Memorable touring experience: *Once spent the night at a Warmshowers host site next door to the East Louisiana State Hospital, an asylum for, among others, the criminally insane. His host cooked up "the best gumbo I ever tasted."*

Hot Tip for a Smooth Trip: *Always carry wet wipes. You can clean your bike, your hands, and even use them in lieu of a shower.*

IT WAS TIME FOR A CHANGE. Right out of college, Stephen Gillan had taken a temp job working on mortgages for a major national bank, but ended up staying for several years — too long.

Dissatisfied, he stockpiled money and resolved to quit and hike the Appalachian Trail. Underprepared, that long walk proved very difficult at first. Still, after three months of agonizing and sorting out logistical problems, "I found out I loved it," he says.

He had joined an elite fraternity within American culture — saturated as it is with TV, obesity, laziness, and drift — of those who fit in by not fitting in.

"They have this passion and they follow it," he says.

Halfway through the trail, he realized that the next logical step was the Pacific Crest Trail. But how to get to the starting point in Southern California? Why not bike, he thought. So he bought a mountain bike off of Craigslist for $100 and flew to Florida.

"I had no idea what I was doing," he says. "I hadn't even really been on a bike since I was 13." Still, "you quit your job...what are you gonna do?"

The answer: About 60 miles per day through Louisiana, Texas, New Mexico and Arizona. Though concerned for his safety on busy roads at first, he soon got into a groove, staying at churches all over the south, then campgrounds as Western public lands became more common.

For Gillan, the trip, along with his subsequent success on the PCT and the mountain-bike-only Continental Divide trail, served as an opportunity to see America and himself in a different light. In the middle of his cross-country touring, he decided his next career move: astrophysics.

These days, he is busy accomplishing that goal, at Colorado State University in Fort Collins.

BENEDICTION

THIS BUSINESS OF BICYCLE TOURING. It's a grand thing, but an all-too-niche pastime. The culture of bicycle racing cluttered up the simple, elegant reality of the tour with neon, Spandex, space age tools, and foil packets of food. But I hope you now agree: This is not rocket science. You don't need to be a gym rat, mechanical genius or heiress to gain entry. That's why I'm looking forward to seeing you, and hopefully increasing numbers of our fellow Americans, out there on the road.

Because whether you know it or not, you yearn for the steady percussion of waters that give life to whatever they touch. You will learn this when waking up beside a churning stream, under the sunrise on a perfect summer morning in a valley in Idaho. May you hear this.

Because you cannot know truly how delicious food is until you work up a ferocious hunger and satisfy it at a roadside fruit stand, doughnut shop, or with that evening's pot of pasta. May you taste this.

Because a rich texture is added to your life when you see that panorama you were not expecting, or catch a glimpse of a mountain lion or bear, or ride through the rain until the sun finally breaks. May you see this.

Because after several days, you will reach down and touch your leg muscles and observe that they have turned to cast iron, the product of many hours of tough, primal work that pumped more endorphins into your brain than you figured was possible. May you feel this.

And because whenever we set out, seeking high adventure, exciting discovery, and new friends, we are bound to find what we're looking for, and so much more. May you live this.

ACKNOWLEDGEMENTS

Many thanks to the editing committee, especially Steve Harrington, Andrew Clouse, Jerry Beaupré, Lindsay Wood, and Dave Bellefeuille-Rice. Also many thanks to the "bike people," Ed Gross, Minnie McMahon, and Stephen Gillan. Finally, thanks to the cougar that prowls around the top of Lolo Pass in Montana, for being awesome.

ALSO BY PETER RICE

Bike Tour New Mexico (Series)
Cheat Sheet: The easy roadmap to smooth and efficient Toastmasters meetings
Drinking Buttermilk: A Eulogy for an American pastime

All titles are available on amazon.com

ABOUT THE AUTHOR

Peter Rice has toured many thousands of miles (in 11 states) and considers that a good start. He lives in Albuquerque with his beloved 30-year-old Trek. A graduate of Colorado College, he has worked as a journalist, electrician, and English teacher. His secret ambition is to ride to the Yukon Territory.

Rice is available for speaking engagements and one-on-one phone consultations. For more information and rates, visit biketournewmexico.com.

STILL HAVE QUESTIONS?

Peter Rice is available for private phone consultations, whether you need planning assistance, a helping hand, or just want to talk strategy about bicycle touring in general (or New Mexico touring in particular). Visit biketournewmexico.com for more information and rates.

Made in the USA
Lexington, KY
28 November 2018